UNWRAPPED

MARVELOUS MUMMIES

ICE MUMMIES

by Joyce Markovics

CHERRY LAKE PRESS

Published in the United States of America by Cherry Lake Publishing Group
Ann Arbor, Michigan
www.cherrylakepublishing.com

Reading Adviser: Marla Conn, MS Ed., Literacy specialist, Read-Ability, Inc.
Content Adviser: Owen Beattie, PhD
Book Designer: Ed Morgan

Photo Credits: © Michele Burgess/Alamy Stock Photo, cover and title page; Public Domain, TOC; © Felix Seichter/Shutterstock, 4–5; © Paul Hanny, 5; © South Tyrol Museum of Archaeology/Dario Frasson, 6; © South Tyrol Museum of Archaeology/Harald Wisthaler, 7; © South Tyrol Museum of Archaeology/Ochsenreiter, 8 top; © Ali Al-Awartany/Shutterstock, 8 bottom; © South Tyrol Museum of Archaeology/EURAC/Samadelli/Staschitz, 9; Public Domain, 10; © Tomas Castelazo, 11; Wikimedia Commons, 12; © Wikimedia Commons, 13; Wikimedia Commons, 14–15; © Michele Burgess/Alamy Stock Photo, 15; Public Domain, 16–17; Wikimedia Commons, Gordon Leggett, 16 bottom; © Owen Beattie, 18; © Owen Beattie, 19; © Owen Beattie, 20–21.

Cherry Lake Press is an imprint of Cherry Lake Publishing Group.

Library of Congress Cataloging-in-Publication Data

Names: Markovics, Joyce L., author.
Title: Ice mummies / by Joyce L Markovics.
Description: Ann Arbor, Michigan : Cherry Lake Publishing, [2021] | Series: Unwrapped: marvelous mummies | Includes bibliographical references and index. | Audience: Ages 8 | Audience: Grades 2-3
Identifiers: LCCN 2020030255 (print) | LCCN 2020030256 (ebook) | ISBN 9781534180420 (hardcover) | ISBN 9781534182134 (paperback) | ISBN 9781534183148 (ebook) | ISBN 9781534181434 (pdf)
Subjects: LCSH: Ice mummies—Juvenile literature.
Classification: LCC GN293 .M353 2021 (print) | LCC GN293 (ebook) | DDC 599.9–dc23
LC record available at https://lccn.loc.gov/2020030255
LC ebook record available at https://lccn.loc.gov/2020030256

Printed in the United States of America
Corporate Graphics

CONTENTS

A FROZEN FIND

The sun was shining on September 19, 1991. Helmut and Erika Simon were enjoying a hike in the snowy Alps. As they walked, they spotted some slush and ice ahead of them. There was "something brown sticking out of the ice," said Helmut.

At first, the couple thought it was garbage left by hikers. But as they got closer, they saw a bald human head and shoulders. "It's a man!" cried Erika.

The body that Helmut and Erika found in the ice

The Simons were hiking in the Tyrolean Alps. This mountain range is between Austria and Italy.

The Simons believed they had found a hiker who had recently died. They quickly made their way to a nearby inn. The couple told the inn's caretaker about their **grim** discovery.

The valley where the ice man was found

The next day, people tried to remove the body from the ice. But it wouldn't budge. The only thing they freed was part of a copper ax. But it was no ordinary ax. The tool was over 5,000 years old!

The 5,000-year-old ax

A bearskin cap and a shoe were also found near the body.

On September 23, 1991, a team freed the body from the ice. The man Helmut and Erika stumbled upon was an **ancient** mummy! He had been frozen in the ice for 5,300 years. The man was nicknamed Ötzi (OOT-zee). He was one of the oldest mummies ever discovered!

What Ötzi might have looked like when he was alive

Scientists soon learned that Ötzi had been shot by a stone arrowhead and bled to death. And he had an old knife wound on his hand. They also found wild goat meat and grains inside his stomach!

A wild goat

Scientists examined every part of Ötzi. They looked at his clothes and belongings, and even inside his body. In doing so, they unlocked secrets about Ötzi's life and **culture**.

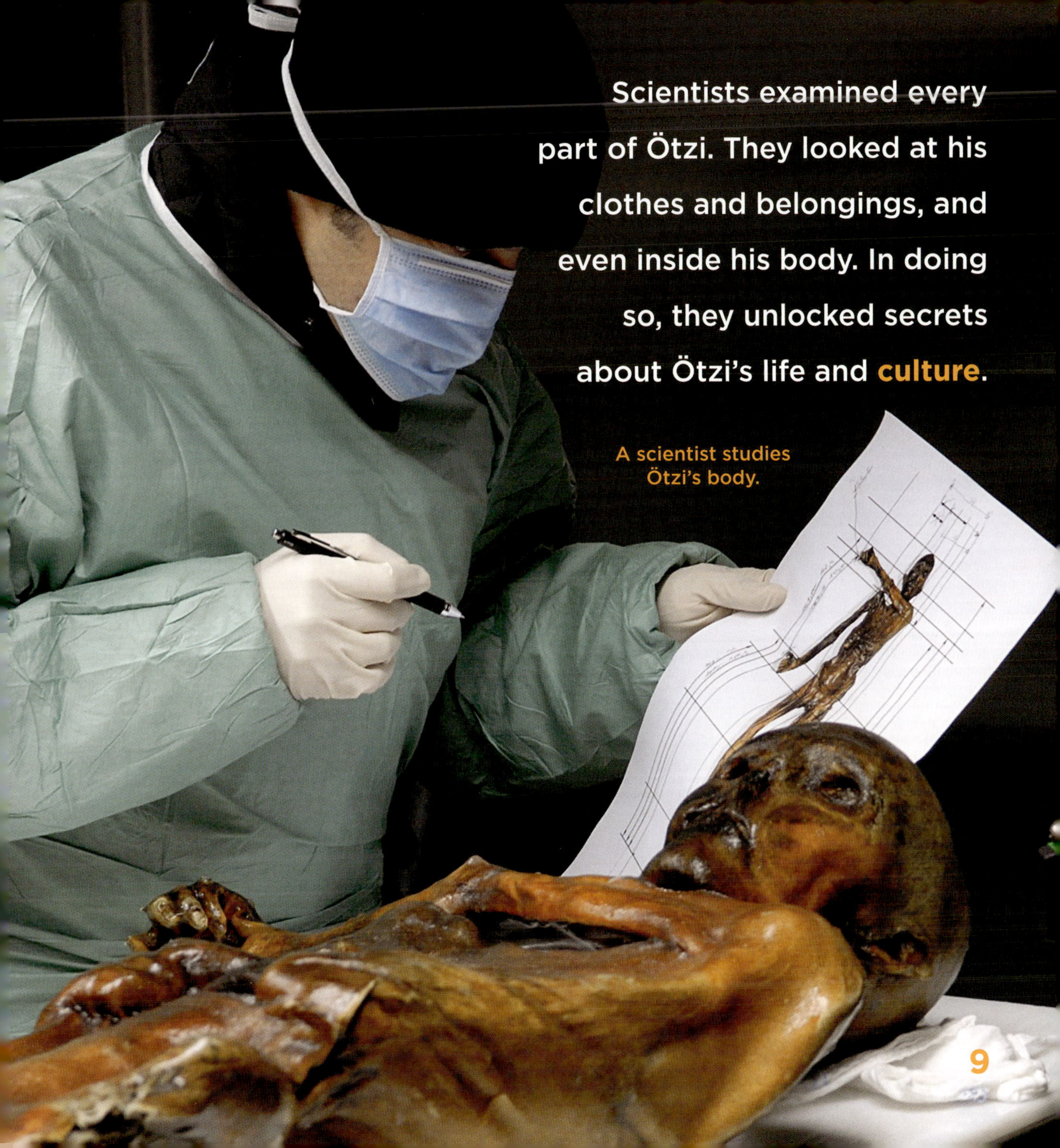

A scientist studies Ötzi's body.

MAKING A MUMMY

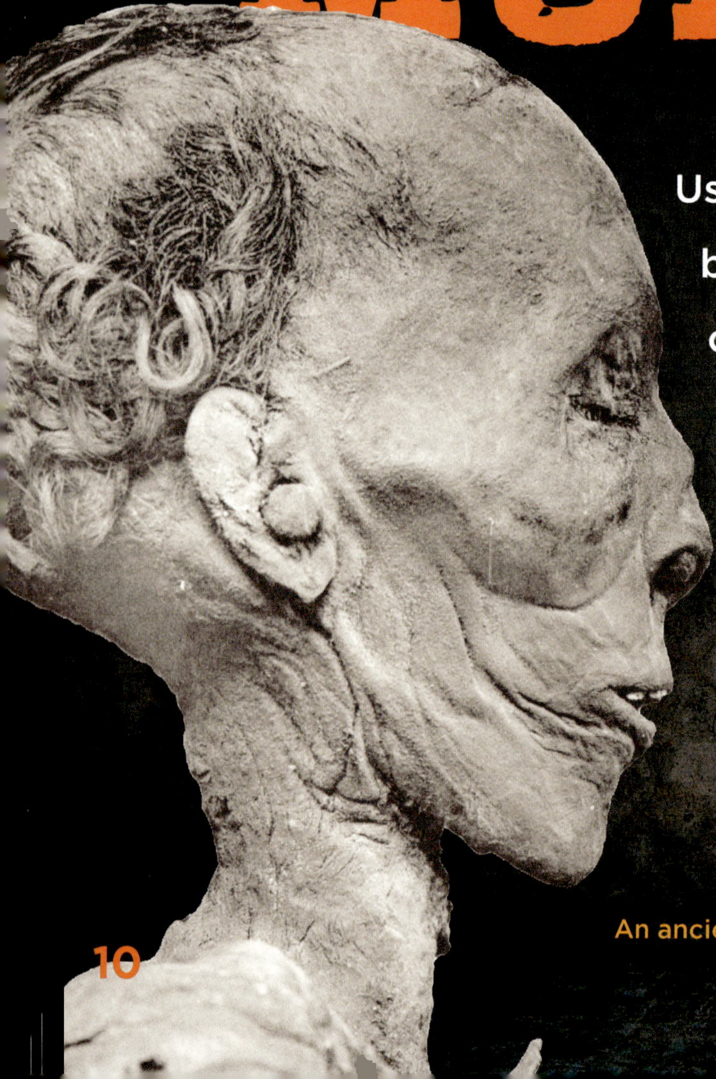

Usually, when a person dies, the body **decays**. Tiny living things called bacteria break down the **flesh**. A mummy is a dead body that has not totally decayed. It may still have skin or other soft **tissue**.

An ancient Egyptian mummy

There are two main ways that mummies form. Sometimes, people create mummies by using chemicals or smoke to **preserve** a dead body. Mummies can also form naturally by drying out before they decay. This is what happened with Ötzi.

This Mexican mummy hand formed naturally in hot, dry weather.

How does an ice mummy form? First, a person has to die in a very cold place. Fewer bacteria grow in icy **climates**. This slows down or stops decay. Then, over a long time, the body dries up. Freeze-drying can preserve dead bodies—sometimes for thousands of years!

Three ice mummy children were found on this mountaintop in South America.

By studying ice mummies, scientists can get a close look at the past. Each mummy tells a special story about a life lived long ago.

Animals can also become ice mummies. This is a 40,000-year-old baby woolly mammoth.

Ice mummies have been found in many chilly parts of the world. These places include Canada, Chile, Greenland, Peru, and Russia.

ARCTIC ICE BABY

In 1972 in Greenland, two brothers made a surprising discovery. They found what they thought was a doll. It was actually a 500-year-old frozen **Inuit** baby.

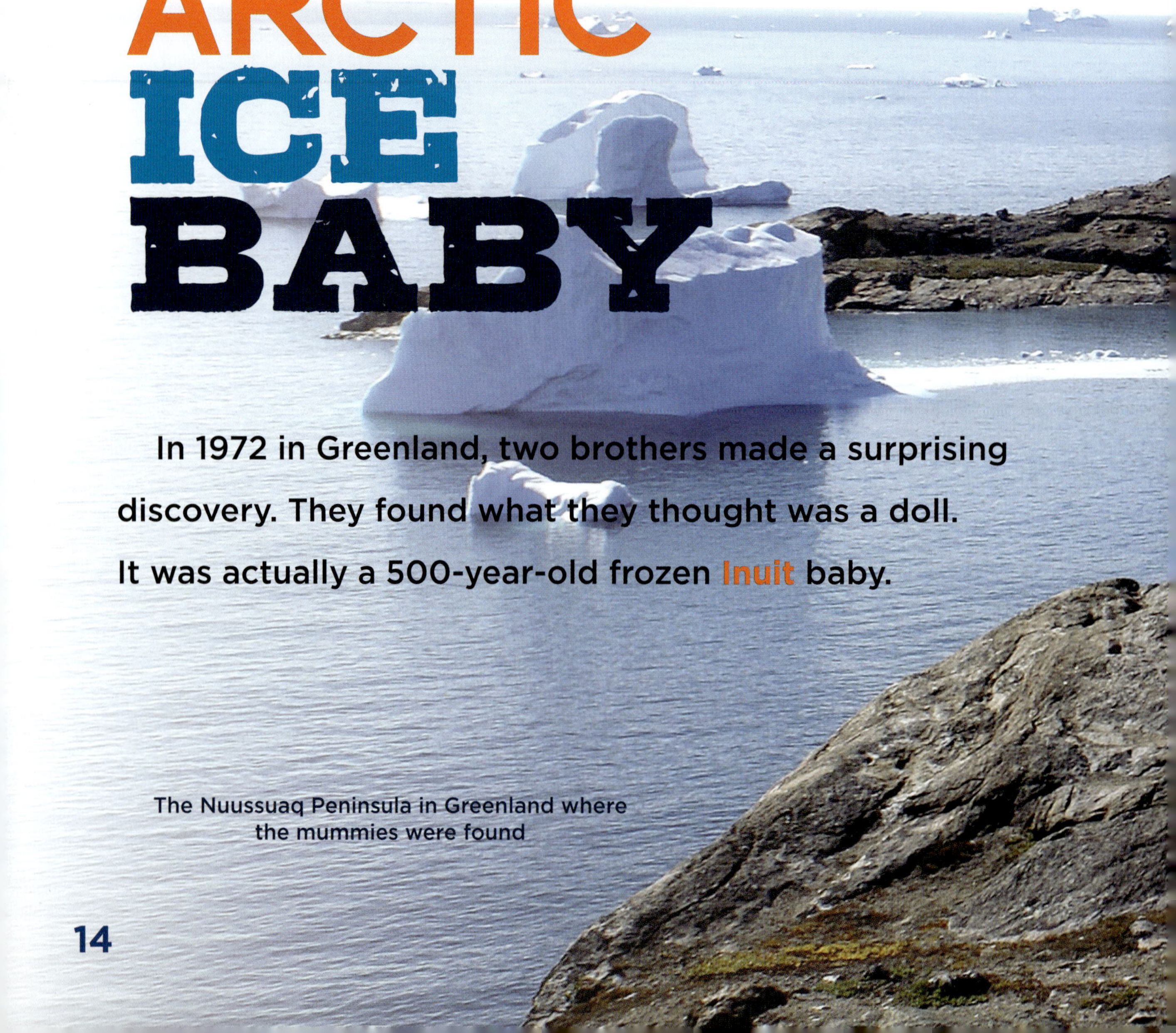

The Nuussuaq Peninsula in Greenland where the mummies were found

The baby was discovered in an icy **tomb** with its mother. There were six other mummies too. All were fully dressed in animal furs. The freezing temperatures and winds had kept the bodies from decaying. Some experts believe that the mother died before the baby. And the baby was possibly buried alive!

The mummy baby was found wearing a tiny sealskin coat.

What happened to the baby? In the past, the Inuit people believed a young child would likely starve without a mother. Experts think that might be why the baby was buried alive.

FROSTY GRAVE

"He's there, he's right there," gasped Arne Carlson. It was 1984 on Beechey Island in Canada. Arne, an **archaeologist**, and scientist Owen Beattie had just made a shocking discovery. They had uncovered a **lifelike** mummy of a sailor. The sailor, John Torrington, died in 1846. He was a part of the doomed Franklin **Expedition**.

John Torrington's grave marker on Beechey Island, Nunavut, Canada

The 1845 Franklin Expedition included two ships from England. Both ships got stuck in ice in the Canadian **Arctic**. All the men aboard eventually died.

Owen wanted to dig up John Torrington to learn exactly how he died. To reach the body, Owen's team hacked through 5 feet (1.5 meters) of **permafrost**. The team then used warm water to thaw John's face and body. Slowly, the sailor's face became **visible**. Amazingly, it looked as if John had just died.

The mummy of John Torrington was found inside this black coffin.

The John Torrington mummy

John's skin was still soft. His eyes were half-opened. The rest of his body and clothing were also perfectly preserved. The permafrost had sealed off his body from the air. It was as if he had been stored in a deep freezer.

The ice mummy helped scientists understand what happened to the men of the Franklin Expedition. It also left them wondering. What other secrets are still frozen in the ice?

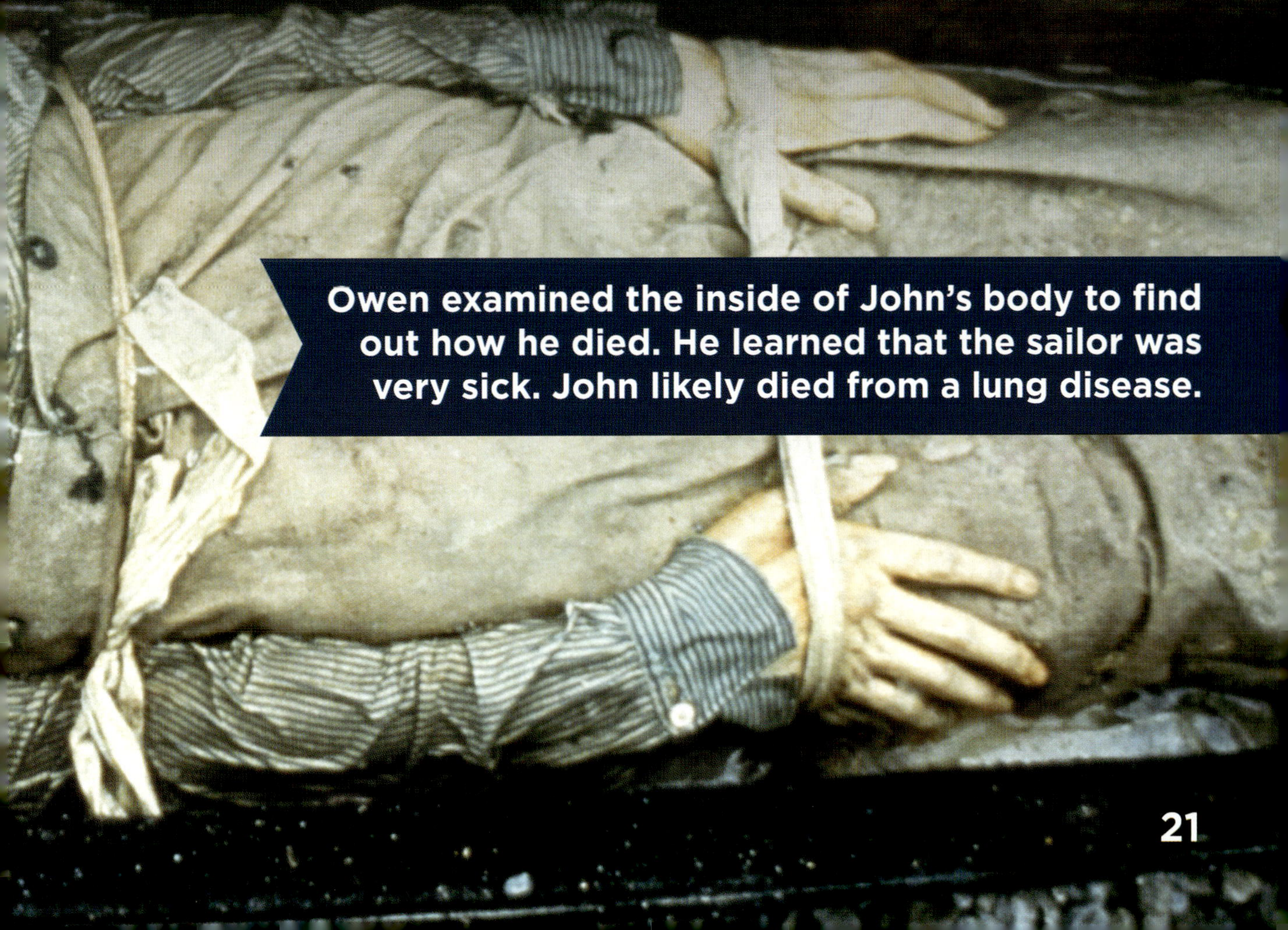

Owen examined the inside of John's body to find out how he died. He learned that the sailor was very sick. John likely died from a lung disease.

MUMMY MAP

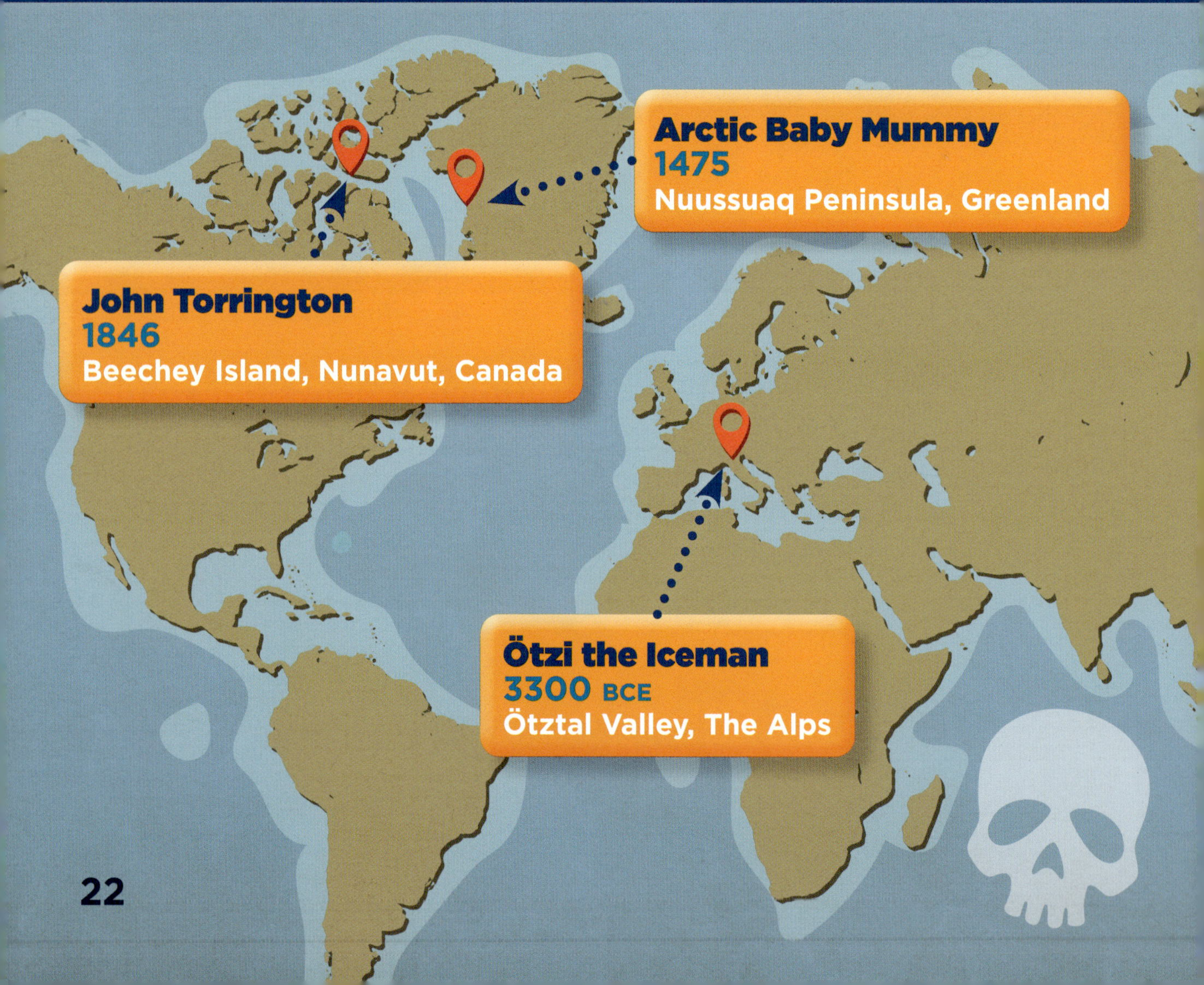
Arctic Baby Mummy
1475
Nuussuaq Peninsula, Greenland
John Torrington
1846
Beechey Island, Nunavut, Canada
Ötzi the Iceman
3300 BCE
Ötztal Valley, The Alps

GLOSSARY

ancient (AYN-shuhnt) very old

archaeologist (ahr-kee-AH-luh-jist) someone who studies the past by digging up and examining old things

Arctic (ARK-tik) the northernmost area on Earth

climates (KLYE-mits) weather conditions over a long period

culture (KUHL-chur) the way of life of a particular people

decays (dih-KAYZ) rots or breaks down

expedition (ek-spuh-DISH-uhn) a long trip taken for a specific reason, such as exploring

flesh (FLESH) the soft part of a body that covers the bones

grim (GRIM) gloomy and unpleasant

Inuit (IN-oo-it) a person or group of people from the Arctic

lifelike (LIFE-like) looking alive or real

permafrost (PUR-muh-frost) a layer of soil that stays frozen throughout the year

preserve (prih-ZURV) to protect something so that it stays in its original state

tissue (TISH-oo) a mass of similar cells that form a particular part of the body

tomb (TOOM) a grave, room, or building for holding a dead body

visible (VIZ-uh-buhl) something that's able to be seen

wound (WOOND) an injury in which the skin is cut

FIND OUT MORE

Books

Carney, Elizabeth. *Mummies*. Washington, D.C.: National Geographic, 2009.

Dubowski, Mark, and Cathy East Dubowski. *Ice Mummy*. New York: Random House, 1998.

Kudalis, Eric. *Ice Mummies: Frozen in Time*. North Mankato, MN: Capstone Press, 2002.

Websites

Secrets of the Ice: Ice Mummies
https://secretsoftheice.com/ice-mummies

South Tyrol Museum of Archaeology: Ötzi the Iceman
http://www.iceman.it/en/the-discovery

Visit Greenland: Qilakitsoq Mummies Show Life and Death
https://visitgreenland.com/about-greenland/qilakitsoq-mummies

INDEX

ABOUT THE AUTHOR

Joyce Markovics digs mummies—and all kinds of curious things. She also loves learning about people from the past and telling their stories.